MW01000468

House Dressing

INTERIORS FOR COLORFUL LIVING

For Leslie —
Color Your World!

♡ Janie

House Dressing

INTERIORS FOR COLORFUL LIVING

JANIE MOLSTER

WRITTEN WITH KATHRYN O'SHEA-EVANS

ℳ

For my children,
John, Robert, Pierre, Swain, and Isabel.

And for my husband, John,
who makes it all come true.

Contents

Introduction

Creating a home that reflects who you are and enhances your life can be a daunting task. Many of my clients begin their projects struggling for direction and inspiration. When they turn to me for advice, I share a secret shortcut I've learned from more than twenty years of experience: look in the mirror. So much can be gleaned about your preferences from how you present yourself to the world. Your handbag, your footwear, your jewelry (or lack thereof)—all are details that tell your story. Whether you are clad from head to toe in gray cashmere or ebullient, sunny hues, your muse may be no further than your own reflection. Hence the title for this book: *House Dressing.*

It's a lesson I learned early on. Long before my design firm had projects featured in national publications and I was fortunate enough to work with some of the best tradespeople in the business, I was steeped in sartorial thrills thanks to my mother, Jane. We lived in a tiny town in rural northeastern North Carolina, yet my mother was always stylish and effortlessly elegant. She brought the same level of aesthetic care to our home, which she festooned in mint greens and pastel pinks. As a child, I often spent Sunday afternoons after church splayed out on a pink Persian rug with my ears glued to the conversations between my mother and her best friend, Ross. They chatted for hours on end about fabrics, colors, fashion, flowers, and travel. On those lazy afternoons, I learned the importance of approaching the world creatively, thinking outside the box, and always striving for originality.

Fast-forward a few decades, and I'm a mother myself, as well as a seasoned designer, and I have dressed and redressed my family's house. We are a raucous group—my husband and I have five children (four sons and a daughter) and now have the added bonus of daughters-in-law and grandchildren. Our houses have always had to be high-performance to stand up to the

On the porch of my 1907 home in Richmond, Virginia. PRECEDING: An antique French settee supplies timeless grace under handmade papier-mâché botanicals. The mod cocktail table, also made of papier-mâché, injects lighthearted levity.

challenge of playgroups, birthday parties, and festive family gatherings. I love to entertain and want our interiors to delight us as well as our guests. Comfort has reigned supreme among our family's design priorities. Our boys always made sure of that, teaching me that if a sofa was long enough for napping and the fabric was soft enough to rest a cheek on, it could be any color in the rainbow (which is how I pulled off so much pink, as you'll see in my home).

My firm is known for blending beauty with harmony and just the right note of surprise. We always make sure that there are inviting places to sit and enjoy the embellishments of a room, which is a game changer for enticing a crowd and ensuring they'll linger. Spending unhurried time in a room is when the subtle details of a well-layered interior reveal themselves: the delicate sheen of a wallcovering, the dense sofa cushions that wrap you like a hug, or the glistening patina of a well-loved table surface. Historic houses and antiques are often in our mix, but we always try to keep our finger on the proverbial pulse of the makers who continue to reinvent and improve our design options. After all, one day our children will be collecting treasures from artisans, circa 2021!

When it comes down to it, designing a memorable home is about grace. I have been blessed with family, friends, and clients who have showered me with grace; I try to give it back with my interiors. Southerners are taught at a young age the importance of a gracious home that makes people feel uplifted. So, I invite you with as much warmth as words will allow into the pages of *House Dressing*. I'm excited to share a few of my favorite houses and give you pathways to create more beauty in your own home.

A centuries-old mirror and walls covered in de Gournay's hand-painted "Whistler Peacocks" pattern add history to this dining room. Making the space modern: a glossy sideboard and intricately beaded lamps. Underfoot, a patterned sisal rug ushers in a less formal note.

Enchanted

MY DESIGN LAB

I was seven months pregnant and teetering on a ladder with a paint roller in my hand when I knew I was a designer. I was only on the second rung—and even then, my husband was furious—but I simply couldn't sleep another night with our apartment being that dusty beige. I certainly wasn't going to bring a baby into its new home surrounded by that hue. You could call it "nesting," but that level of obsession about interiors simply wasn't normal for an English major like me, and my calling as an interior designer was suddenly whispering in my ear.

Soon after, in the first home we ever owned, a Federal-style brick row house in Richmond, Virginia's Fan District, friends would shuffle through and their eyes would widen. Back then, I was long on ideas and short on expendable funds, and I adorned our house the best way I could. I had a zebra-print carpet and deep pink walls—even today, I maintain that a fresh paint color can transform a room. I made voluminous floor-to-ceiling drapes with washed linen that would billow like a cream puff ball gown in a strong breeze. In a hallway, I hung a collection of vintage mirrors from trompe l'oeil roping; it was our own diminutive version of the Hall of Mirrors at Versailles. Friends would come over to ask for design advice, then prod me for my services in their own homes. On my next birthday, when a group of them got together and had business cards printed for me, my fate as a designer was sealed.

My own Richmond, Virginia, dining room is instantly welcoming, thanks to a ceiling painted in an abstract pink pattern and pair of Italian candelabras reflected in antiqued mirrors.
PRECEDING: Reigning supreme in the foyer: a beloved 1920s chinoiserie secretary. Purchased in my early twenties, it remains a favorite and echoes my mantra: "Buy what you love and it will always work."
OVERLEAF: Walls covered in gray silk are a calming foil for a profusion of pink embellishments.

My collection of vintage Italian papier-mâché trays found a fitting perch in the secretary. OPPOSITE: In the foyer, a wall of art from my collection. The various styles provide instant interest, and differing mediums are cohesive when limited to my go-to palette of black, white, and gray.

Now, with my firm long established, I spend my days creating elevated, evolving interiors that are also approachable. There is no room for intimidation in design, least of all in a home, the place we retire to each night for much-deserved R & R with the people we love most. I don't want to have any areas that are off-limits, whether for clients who have blue-chip art collections or those whose toddlers are running around with Sharpies. My advice: don't wait to live your life. If having beautiful things is in your purview, buy them now—not when the puppy has grown, or your son is no longer plodding across the carpet in muddy shoes. Life will never be pristine. If it's not your teenager in cleats, it's your husband drinking pinot noir on the white sofa, or your friends getting rowdy with the lo mein.

When I start the design process with new clients, the first thing I tell them is: This process is about you. When we're done, a stranger could walk through your house and feel like they know you. This home will tell your story. That's always been my goal in our current home, a 1907 Richmond foursquare farmhouse that we've lived in for twenty years. It exemplifies my personal aesthetic in every inch, as it should; it's been my de facto design laboratory for two decades.

The house has humble origins. It's settled so much over the last century that a marble doesn't just roll across the floor, it's like you've shot it—hard. With the character that age brings and the absence of a plumb line, the place has an *Alice in Wonderland* quality that allows for free-range experimentation. The one thing you can expect in every room is to see something unexpected. There are opulent moments, such as the dining room's eighteenth-century

Blousy peonies seem to burst like fireworks from within a favorite vase, my mother's champagne cooler. OVERLEAF: Comfort rules in the living room, which I separated into two spaces: one for intimate chats around the fireplace, and the other with two pale-pink sofas that are notably roomy for my tall sons in need of a TV binge. Free-flowing above it all are beadboard ceilings studded with exposed beams and a custom chandelier with cylindrical crystals in my favorite pink hues.

In my house, every room is a living room, built for all the glory and chaos of real life.

Limiting pattern in this sitting area, I opted instead to add interest with wide, contrasting curtain banding at eye level. An antique column injects a corner with a good dose of age and patina, while a fringed leather footstool brings an extra serving of fun.

Original pine floors are stained a pale blond as a backdrop for the lively color palette. Employing various textures helps a room feel layered and collected. OPPOSITE: An antique gilt mirror crowned with a working clock is an eye-catching focal point between a pair of Giacometti-inspired sculptures that I had converted into lamps. Pink stripes painted on the wall give age-old antiques, like these zinc wall baskets, a fresh backdrop.

I remember my grandmother's kitchen— there was no island, just a kitchen table in the center of the room. I love that people can come in, sit down, and visit while you're cooking.

A painted floor pattern is one of my favorite ways to add graphic punch. Here, it grounds the kitchen in lieu of an area rug. Striated grass cloth wallpaper meanders from the walls onto the Sub-Zero refrigerator panels, providing a prismatic backdrop for an effervescent bubble light fixture.

When clients worry that they're attracted to design styles that are all over the map, I have to laugh. One of my hallmarks is corralling my multiple design personalities: the more, the merrier.

antique console tables, nabbed in the South of France, and the gleaming moss-green lacquered den. But there are also less serious, impromptu moments, like the inexpensive paper lantern I suspended over the dining table after a client fell for my long-standing antique Italian fragment chandelier. In the living room, color-blocked curtains inject one of my favorite colors—pink—without locking me into a pattern. Across the room, whitewashed Giacometti-esque sculptures retrofitted as floor lamps flank a giltwood antique settee. There's a note of sunset-pastel bands in the wallpaper that lines our kitchen and, yes, we wrapped it over the refrigerator doors. With the right wallpaper, just about any surface is fair game.

Ultimately, I want people to have fun with their homes. There has to be something irreverent and playful and wrong in each room. When it's all perfect, the first thing I do is mess it up a little bit. Life is for living.

An antique chest with inlaid marquetry detailing and a much-loved carved putto (wooden cherub) have an au courant edge in this mossy-green living space. It's my family's go-to hangout spot in winter, when the gas fireplace flickers at the touch of a button.

Sundry patterns in
various colorways are
united in the lush green
of this sitting room,
where the wall color
jibes with the verdant
scene beyond the
windows. Keeping the
space garden-fresh is
sculptural seating,
including a rattan swivel
chair and a low-slung
fireside perch by
Jonathan Adler.

There are endless shades of pink, which melds easily with many other palettes. Paired with the right strong elements, its femininity can be quieted. Remember, furnishings and friends always look rosier in a pink glow.

A high-gloss, watermelon-hued paint offers a perfect foil for gauzy black-and-white curtains and a red-and-white-striped antique "throne" settee in a sunny bay window. A concrete footed table provides an edgy contrast. I discovered the Moroccan rug in a remote village in the Atlas Mountains.

Graphic white and black accessories, such as curvy Murano glass lamps and iron-based barrel chairs, soften the candy-colored maximalism of this sitting room. An X-bench upholstered in faux fur serves as both a footstool and cocktail table. The '70s-era rug was found in Marrakech.

In the bedroom I share with my husband, more is definitely more. A vintage *suzani* is draped behind the silk-velvet headboard, and topped with an antique candelabra, turning the entire wall into a maximalist focal point. Elaborately embroidered silk curtains are balanced by a nearly threadbare Oushak rug. OVERLEAF: A black-and-white color scheme on the porch allows the garden greenery to take center stage.

The New Formal

"Pretty" is almost a bad word in the design world, which tends to gravitate toward what's in vogue. I'll let you in on a secret. Unlike fickle trends, a room that is truly pretty and quietly elegant will always stand the test of time. Densely knotted carpets, timeworn gilding, glistening crystal, and luxurious fabrics never date or go out of style. The reason? Dressy doesn't have to be stuffy, and elegance doesn't have to be staid. The New Formal isn't just for ladies' lounges or pompous parlors.

A formal room has several trademarks. For one, it doesn't skimp. There's an expression: "The higher the hair, the closer to God." Ample curtains are similarly heavenly. Curtains don't need to be silk taffeta damask, but they do need to be voluminous and expertly constructed. We hang them well above the top of the window, at the base of the crown molding, and fabricate them at a minimum of two-and-a-half times the window's volume. Custom dressmaker detailing, such as small accordion-pleated ruffles, embroidery along the leading edge, and passementerie embellishments, further enhance the ethereal effect.

In putting together the components of a room embracing the New Formal, I abide by an age-old design maxim: maintain a nice mix of skirts and legs. Skirted sofas or an ottoman upholstered to the floor should be balanced by a few exposed tables or chair legs. When a lovely little leg is de rigueur, my go-to is often a seventeenth- or eighteenth-century settee in a giltwood finish, which adds an aura of peerage grandeur.

Antiques are a must for an evolved formal room. Often providing an interesting backstory, an antique can magically elevate the sense of place in a room. Once, I proposed a century-old Anatolian Oushak rug to clients, and they hesitated. "We live hard in our house," they said.

Simplifying the elegant entrance hall of this 1777 Virginia country estate are an eighteenth-century unfinished-wood trumeau mirror and a seventeenth-century settee left covered in a casual, dressed-down muslin. Also offering a fresh contrast and a little carefree ambience is the oversized, mellowed-gold carriage lantern, more typically found in an outdoor application in a house of this age and stature.

OPPOSITE: An antique Swedish cabinet has pride of place in the foyer, its authentic weathered finish mirrored by two of the owner's collection of French barometers, a nod to the area's Huguenot settlers. A painting by artist Steven Cushner enlivens the scene.
ABOVE: Intricately patterned wallcovering unites this home's multiple palatial passageways.

OPPOSITE: In the showstopping central hallway, Louis XVI chairs are covered in a coral medallion fabric with a hand-painted quality. The punch lent by an antique Turkish rug serves up the same energy that colorful throw pillows might. ABOVE: For a tailored effect, I had these draperies edged in accordion-pleated fabric, a dressmaker detail that begs to be touched. OVERLEAF: On a sofa skirted in a contrasting jute fringe, a rustic fiber is used in a highly refined way.

In the dining room of the country estate, the geometry of a wheel-backed dining chair is showcased against hand-painted Gracie wallpaper. OPPOSITE: When using a scenic wallpaper, I turn the volume down on other elements. To that end, I selected a quiet sisal carpet and draped the table in simple cotton paisley. The seventeenth-century chandelier has a flurry of pink and green glass flowers throughout.

I reminded them that the rug was made before they were born, and will likely be around long after they're gone. The same is true for antique furniture, which, when properly chosen, can be equally durable.

We've moved on from the fragile, practically cordoned-off living rooms of our childhoods. I'm a believer in filling your house with beautiful things and then actually using them. Ideally every room is a "living" room and built for real life. In fact, many of my clients who would seem to lean toward "casual" or "masculine" design can find themselves drawn to a more elegant room if the correct design formula is used: provide plenty of inviting seating, accessible surfaces, soft lighting, and a pretty object or two. My goal scenario is simple: My client walks down a hallway in his house and glances into a sunny room with heavily fringed curtains and a gleaming crystal chandelier. He notices a deeply cushioned chair, an ottoman nearby, and a table by the window that offers a nice space for a laptop and a cup of coffee. Lo and behold, there's a phone charger in the wall plug. Intrigued, he sits down, a few hours pass, and he realizes he's spent the afternoon enjoying the most beautiful, elegant room in his house.

In a Windsor Farms, Richmond, family home, two antique hand-carved candle sconces flank a modern metallic painting and cast an ethereal luminescence come nightfall. The streamlined, bench-seated sofa eliminates the visual clutter of multiple seat cushions and allows decorative pillows in embossed velvet to shine.

KEITH LANGHAM

MODERN WOMEN

ABOUT DECORATING

PORTRAITS OF COURAGE

bby McAlpine THE HOME WITHIN US

SECOND BLOOM

OCATIVE INTERIORS · RAY BOOTH

Comfort is king, even in the prettiest room of the house—which is why these homeowners can lounge in swiveling fireside chairs and easily prop their feet atop an ottoman. OPPOSITE: I might be known for my use of color, but I also enjoy executing quiet, serene spaces. These window treatments are grand in scale but simple in material: a linen-cotton blend, with a Greek key banding on the leading edge for a tailored finish.

The principal bedroom of this South Florida bungalow has a lavish feel, thanks to a custom velvet headboard in an Art Deco–inspired silhouette, and serpentine-fronted end tables in a silver finish. Still, it's not too precious, thanks to bubble mirrors and free-flowing window treatments with an appliqué edge.

Glamorous

A CAPTIVATING GEORGIAN

T here's a reason aesthetes have fever dreams of Paris, and it's not just the thought of a note-perfect *pain au chocolat*. It's the joie de vivre that's visible in nearly everything, from the radiant Beaux Arts architecture to the gilt statues at every turn. In short, it's the glamour, as palpable as mist rising on the Seine. When I began designing my clients' late-1920s Georgian estate, sitting proudly at the crest of their riverside property, I approached it with a Francophile's mindset and championed refined maximalism and quality above all else.

The house was a shell when I first walked through it, and the vacant but lovely rooms set the tone for extravagance. Take the formal living room, which emits the vibe of an Art Deco—era Parisian salon. Eyes closed, I could easily conjure a cinematic reel of soft lighting, heated conversations, and the tinkling of champagne coupes. Given the room's classical molding and paneling, I knew we would need to give a nod to the past and showcase exceptional antiques. At the same time, I'm a modernist at my core, and my like-minded clients agreed that the house would also need to reflect our joint leanings.

The bones of the living room necessitated a robust dedication to pull together one-of-a-kind pieces: Murano glass lamps, reverse-painted trumeau mirrors, and curtains with a leading edge of appliqué. The gilt iron branch chandelier, dripping in quartz crystals, made for a fabulous piece of ceiling jewelry. Talk about eye candy! The ultimate glamorous move is to opt for over-the-top luxury in every detail, so the quality reveals itself slowly as you spend time there. In the

Wallpaper can dramatically transform a room, as in this foyer, where an abstract pattern makes a statement, even in a sedate color palette. PRECEDING: An antique Italian sunburst imparts a warm welcome. Balancing all the history supplied by a Swedish settee and antique Turkish rug are fringed leather sconces and cement orb sculptures. OVERLEAF: The living room is a de facto salon, complete with moments of poetry in the form of extremely artful pieces: a pearlescent custom cowhide rug and a chandelier of dangling quartz crystals.

A pair of reverse-painted trumeau mirrors visually expands the living room. Curvaceous occasional tables in the style of legendary designer John Dickinson flank the sinuous sofa. The equally wavy coffee table in a gleaming finish unites the entire space.

In addition to adding instant warmth, gold is pure eye candy. Like my favorite bonbons, I vary the flavors—mixing gilt antiques with sleek lighting and organic, sculptural forms.

dining room, decorative painters worked their magic, applying to the ceiling a waxed plaster finish flecked with gold leaf. Here, heavy lambrequins and dusty damask curtains were out, and airy linen curtains were in. Linen curtains may seem simple enough, but with the fabric dyed a peony-dipped ombré, they become a megawatt moment.

Throughout the home, artful additions have the creatively invigorating effect of a stay at a Left Bank hotel. In the den, punched-metal Moroccan orbs dangle like disco balls, catching the light alongside the gleaming peacock-blue walls. A powder room's splashy floral walls seem watercolored—all the better for making the custom, 1920s-inspired gold vanity pop. A dressed-up paper lantern hangs in the foyer, counterbalancing the weighty charcoal-gray cement spheres that seem to have errantly rolled under the stairs. The element of surprise makes these sculptural shapes even more bewitching.

Given that this is truly a family home, we selected pieces that were solid and durable. This is a busy group, with free-range kids that can access every square inch. Thanks to the evolution of performance fibers that resist wear and tear, gorgeous materials like luxe velvet, airy linen, and iridescent silk convey glamour and keep those rooms accessible and welcoming to every generation, equally child-friendly and parent-approved.

I prefer to landscape rooms with elements of varying heights and volumes, just as one would with garden plantings. In this space, an eighteenth-century marble-topped table is higher than the sofa's seat. Gold spire sconces are mounted on either side of a painting by Charleston artist Kate Long Stevenson. The ceiling, lacquered in a mirror-like white, is nearly phosphorescent.

Decorative painters adorned the waxed plaster ceiling of this dining room with flecks of gold leaf. The space's pièce de résistance: linen curtains in a delicious peony ombré. Comparative quiet reigns elsewhere with gray velvet–upholstered square-backed dining chairs and blond floors, kept bare. The dining table is a whitewashed antique from Sweden; the custom lamps are by Paul Schneider.

Take the time to develop the subtle embellishments of a room so that they all carry equal weight. You want each piece to be like your favorite guest at a cocktail party — lively, but one who never overpowers the conversation.

In the wet bar, the butterscotch quartz counters and backsplash virtually glow in real life. Bench-made cabinetry with doors inset with brass detailing picks up the golden colors in the adjacent stone. The glass orb light fixture wrapped with brass arms is by Hector Finch.

Rings of handblown glass in this custom pendant cast a creative light on this already artful powder room adjacent to the wet bar. OPPOSITE: Paging Art Deco obsessives: the room's ribbed gold sink vanity was custom-made and gleams against overscale, watercolor-style floral wallpaper.

When I have a rug made by our go-to weavers in Morocco, there's great excitement when it arrives. The weavers often take a bit of creative license with my designs and I'm always thrilled with the results — it's what makes it art.

After dark, this den transforms into a cocoon. The light of the fire casts beautiful patterns on saturated teal walls, courtesy of a punched-brass Moroccan light fixture. An organically shaped coffee table and exceedingly plush seating make for an exotic and cozy lair.

I opted for silk draperies
in the same hue as the walls
to maximize the enveloping
aesthetic. As always,
texture reigns supreme: note
the chair at right, its arms
dripping with leather fringe,
and the custom-made
brass chain mail side table.

Seeded-glass pendant
lights illuminate the waterfall
island and perfectly book-
matched marble walls.
A brass band in a living finish
that will mellow over time
trims the plaster hood. The
bar stools are sheathed in
top-stitched leather, an exacting
detail that is reminiscent
of a couture pocketbook.

Suspended from the breakfast room's vaulted ceiling, a brass chandelier with milk glass globes and dripping golden chains has the eye-catching impact of jewelry.
OPPOSITE: A rustic oval table and natural fiber dining chairs bring the space down to earth.
OVERLEAF: Black French doors and window sashes frame the serene river view beyond.

The owners' bedroom has the aesthetic of 1950s Hollywood, from the dramatic custom floor-to-ceiling velvet headboard to the lustrous satin draperies and roman shades. OVERLEAF, FROM LEFT: The table lamps are handblown amber glass. Bedside tables are made of reverse-painted pink glass, framed in brass.

A crystal chandelier above the
deep soaking tub, and mirrored
paneled doors that bounce
back the light boost the sex
appeal in the owners' bath.
Inset mirrors above the vanity
also double the illumination of
Art Deco–inspired sconces.

OPPOSITE: Pom-pom—edged curtains, a feminine tufted headboard, a shearling and Lucite bench, and pink adornments galore enhance the sweetness of the younger sister's room. ABOVE: What little girl wouldn't want such a fantastical bedside lamp?

OPPOSITE: In the older sister's room, a feather-covered orb light fixture, hung from a lavender ceiling, adds a diaphanous touch over the 1940s-inspired bed. ABOVE: An artist was commissioned to create a painting above the fireplace featuring some of the daughter's favorite things, including butterflies, in a palette of aquas and acidic greens.

I love having children involved in the decor of their rooms. I may give a gentle nudge in an overall direction, but the ownership that comes from being a part of the process leaves little ones with more respect for their special spaces.

The sisters share this playroom, complete with Dalmatian-dotted wallpaper, built-in bunks for sleepovers, and a table for art projects and game nights. The frames on the gallery wall easily pop open so they can swap out their featured paintings as time goes on.

With utilitarian aspects tucked away in custom cabinetry, the mudroom's strong elements
each hold their own, including Crayola-bright rugs made in Morocco's Atlas Mountains and
a carved-stone console. OPPOSITE: Wooden veneer wallpaper in a herringbone pattern
covers the ceiling. I chose to center a simple wide stripe on the upholstered benches to allow
the more resounding pieces, including a pair of artichoke-shaped chandeliers, to captivate.

Sutherland's iconic John Dickinson coffee table centers the outdoor living room. A handmade, garden-appropriate copper light fixture hangs from the vaulted ceiling. OVERLEAF: Mixing materials in natural colors and fibers offers depth but allows Mother Nature's ever-changing palette to prevail.

Jute placemats set an earthy tone on the tablescape, allowing bursting bouquets of dahlias and white anemones their moment in the sun. OPPOSITE: Sculptural seating by Janus et Cie is ultra inviting when topped with a soft sheepskin.

Color My World

Picture a world without color. Bursting freshly cut peonies in gray scale, autumn leaves rendered "blah" by dreary monotone. A little sad, right? People think of color as a primarily visual experience, but in truth, it's so much more than that. Color can affect us psychologically as much as anything else. For me, the artist Paul Klee said it best: "Color possesses me. I don't have to pursue it. It will possess me always, I know it." In the interior designer's toolbox, color is a dynamo. We can rev it up, calm it down, and test endless pairings to achieve the perfect combination.

When my firm begins working with new clients, one of the first things we do is assess what we call their "color tolerance." Occasionally people will walk into our office and say, "I'm obsessed with color. Let's do bold, strong color *everywhere*." Sometimes I'll advise caution if I've already noted their wardrobe propensity toward black, white, and an occasional greige. When you're picking your hues, look for the tried and true—the color that dominates your handbag, or your wardrobe, or your car. Why? People have their go-to colors from the day they're born. If you've always loved yellow, it's unlikely you'll wake up fifteen years later and abhor it. I have an abiding fascination with color and all the little intricacies of how to use it in interiors. I remember being given carte blanche to redo my bedroom at age eleven. The thought of the red-and-white gingham ruffled curtains and thick red shag carpeting I chose still makes me smile today. I haven't used the combination of those design elements since then, but I still love a pop of red and am completely besotted with its gentler, more soft-spoken sister, pink.

To design a color-rich room that isn't overwhelming, it's vital to get the balance of color right. If there is a strong splash of color, whether it be on the walls, or curtain fabric, or artwork, you can ensure equilibrium by mirroring that daring color elsewhere in the room in a smaller way.

An abstract painting by artist Lindsay Cowles holds special meaning to the clients and provides a vibrant muse for the living room of their Florida vacation home. Vintage 1970s glass lamps and pillow fabrics echo the rich color palette. OVERLEAF: Flanked by symmetrical arched openings, a grouping from the homeowners' art collection sings against a tranquil backdrop of whites and grays in a classic shingled five-over-four.

For example, a note of a repeated color in a pillow, or a custom fabric lampshade, or an indulgent cashmere throw can create connections throughout the room. Another favorite tactic is staying within a color family in a room, and using varying gradations of intensity and hue in the same range—say, cobalt down to sky blue.

Achieving the most dramatic change can be done in a flash with the right hue, and the beauty of a gallon of paint is that it's not a huge investment. Never rely solely on paint chips; test the color before you take the plunge. My personal strategy is to paint big swatches of two coats on a few walls, each three or four feet wide, so you can see the purity of the color. Remember that color can be a chameleon over the course of a day, so look at it in the morning, afternoon, and evening light to confirm you truly love it.

The most important thing about color is how it makes you feel. I recently designed a living room with an apricot-colored antique secretary, framed by color-blocked curtains in butterscotch and tawny pink, all counterbalanced with sedate gray walls and sugar-white seating. My client gave me the best compliment: "I feel like this room is giving me a hug."

In a Florida bungalow, a classic wallpaper pattern and a buttoned-up dining table become edgy with the addition of lime-green ombré curtains and a red lacquer chinoiserie console. OVERLEAF: Like a sculptural installation, the 1970s molded acrylic table grabs attention and sparks conversations in a contemporary home near Washington, DC. The abstract landscape painting is by artist Karen Blair.

You don't have to look much further than an orchid to see that plum pinks and greens are perfect color complements. OPPOSITE: Paired with a shaggy Turkish rug, velvet curtains the same hue as Beaujolais wine have a decidedly bohemian spirit. OVERLEAF: A little bit of yellow goes a long way; dotting it throughout this space was pivotal for creating a cohesive look.

A painting by artist Ryan McGinness drives the decorative elements in this living space, and is surrounded by Bunny Williams lamps topped with apple-green shades, and sculptural vessels mounted on Lucite brackets. The artwork visible in the room beyond is by artist Alex Katz.

When an erudite client craves a man cave, details take precedence. Here, the requisite oriental rug and leather sofa in toasty caramel are punctuated with contoured brass cocktail tables. The Arne Jacobsen Egg chair is paired with a vintage rattan console. OPPOSITE: A cocktail bar tucked behind folding doors has multiple brass surfaces, including the bar counter, metal grills inset into cabinet doors, and geometric wallcovering.

OPPOSITE: I spotted the apricot-painted secretary in the window of an antique store and it formed the basis of this room's color palette. ABOVE: An antique tapestry and equally age-old settee are freshened up with a crisp linen slipcover and cheery pillow. OVERLEAF: When my client and I fell in love with two curtain fabrics, we decided to use both, switching colors at eye level for graphic impact. Below a mirrored coffee table, a bohemian Turkish *tulu* rug defines the seating space.

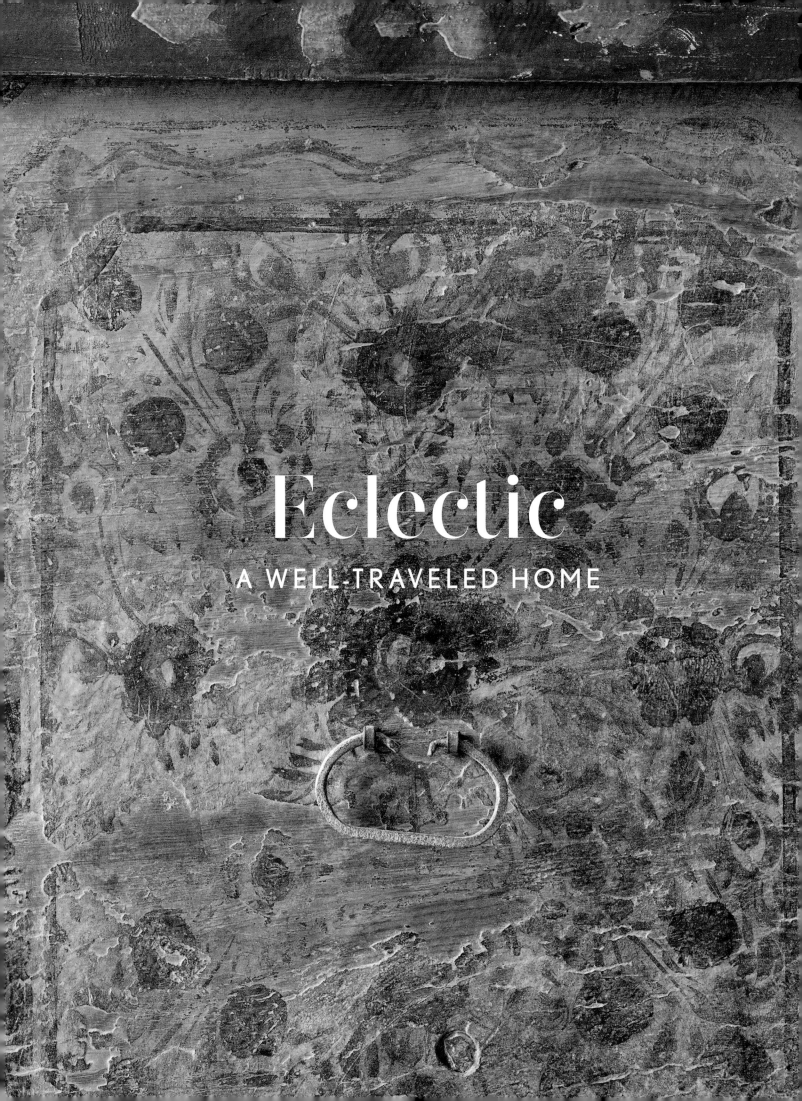

Eclectic

A WELL-TRAVELED HOME

The spellbinding feeling you get when you travel—when you're awestruck by fresco ceilings here, redolent citrus groves there—is very possible to recreate in a home, especially if you approach your interiors with the same sense of unbridled wonder. My clients, a pair of hard-working doctors with an international background and three young children, were feeling a bit of wanderlust. So, we approached the design of their home with escapism and adventure in mind, recreating the electrifying thrills of vagabonding, right within the walls of their Virginia cottage.

To create an eclectic mood, we culled sundry pieces with far-flung roots: a horn chandelier made in South Africa for the dining room, a custom rug handwoven in Morocco in the family room, and even a modernist, fur-clad chair in the primary bedroom. In a single space, the elements may seem unrelated, but there are subtle connectors that create unity. In the dining room, bold, hand-blocked curtain fabric in charcoal and white harmonizes with the bolder color range of the horn chandelier. Walls in varying shades of pink envelope the space in warmth, and dining chairs in a complementary toned velvet offer a hip take on the classic klismos style. Together, they're all so much more transporting than they would be independently.

It helped that the wife has an old soul and an abiding passion for antiques. We went straight to the hunt, giving a beloved seventeenth-century Italian coffer and a French painted mirror pride of place in the foyer. Well-worn antiques all have a story in their bones, and can

Pivotal pieces—including a seventeenth-century Flemish verdure tapestry, a channeled pink sofa, and punched-metal-draped side tables—transform a living room into a salon meant for lingering. PRECEDING: Illuminated by a second-floor window, a dramatic light fixture is suspended above the foyer. The eighteenth-century French settee is especially regal in emerald silk linen upholstery, and finds a fitting neighbor in a seventeenth-century Italian coffer.

Overhead in the salon, a Beaux Arts–inspired hand-plastered ceiling pattern provides the perfect counterbalance to a contemporary light fixture and mossy green silk curtains.

OPPOSITE: Various shades of pale pink envelope the ceiling, walls, and niches, to maximal color effect. Meanwhile, hand-blocked curtains seem to tumble like a waterfall from the fourteen-foot-pitched ceiling.
ABOVE: Providing structure to one wall of the dining room are an antique trumeau mirror from the South of France and a maple sideboard displaying a trio of sculptural totems by artist Julie Silvers.

Pattern play abounds with the parquet wood tabletop and herringbone blond oak flooring. OPPOSITE: Magnifying strength in the space, a tonal horn chandelier cascades from the ceiling. Dining chairs bring a modern silhouette in a coordinating blush velour, and five-foot-tall twinkling glass sconces flank the fireplace.

transport you back to the moment you discovered a treasured find, whether meandering through a beguiling old souk or Les Puces.

Similar to investing in a piece of original art, there's much to learn when beginning to create a home with a collected look of personality-driven pieces, and it's never too early, or too late, to start your education. Whether you have found your forever house or live a more migratory lifestyle, start the process of learning what you love, and study the difference between what is "pretty good" and a treasured find. Every time I go antiquing, I discover something new about how an object is made, where to find the subtle clues on provenance and age, or how to suss out whether a piece has had extensive repair. I also inevitably begin to develop trusting and invaluable relationships with dealers. The best dealers love to teach, whether you're a serious buyer or you're just trying to learn. Cultivating connections and friendships with these savvy purveyors has landed me those thrilling calls from their buying trips with "Look what I found!" and "I know you love these!"

Those relationships come in especially handy when you're designing an eclectic home like this one. In lieu of an archetypal living room, we created a space that feels more like a sexy lounge in a boutique hotel—a transporting escape for busy parents needing a deep breath. All the disparate elements of the room commingle like well-heeled guests from every corner of the globe: peridot-green taffeta window treatments, a pastoral Flemish tapestry with the requisite threadbare portions, and, adding a much-needed bite amidst the moody sophistication, a contemporary channeled tourmaline-pink sofa. Anchored by

Casting a party-ready glow over this kitchen's washed-oak island are twin light fixtures by midcentury designer Gaetano Sciolari.
OVERLEAF: A sixty-six-inch couture range by Lacanche sets the tone for the cook space and is balanced by the custom stone hood and backsplash.

the casual texture of a sisal rug, each item feels grounded. In the family room, an earthy effect takes hold with pillows in Kuba-inspired fabrics. A plush custom rug in tawny hues warms the space with rich caramel, mocha, and saffron.

The principal bedroom is a consummate sanctuary, with ombré velvet curtains and exotic agate table lamps. A glamorous gold-framed canopy bed practically commands my client to don a marabou-trimmed dressing gown. Yet, moving through these rooms doesn't feel disjointed. They share a common thread of evolution. Each room began with a design element that was so beautiful or unique that it caused us to stop in our tracks. Whether it's the dining room's dramatic hand-blocked curtains, or the principal bedroom's regal canopy bed, or the pair of 1970s-era Gaetano Sciolari chandeliers over the kitchen island, signature pieces led the way for the design formula that followed. The rooms flow together like music. Each has a different tone, but with the unified "beat" of the furniture, finishes, art, and accessories, they make a song you want to hear over and over.

In the breakfast room, vintage Savonarola campaign chairs in their original emerald-green velvet slings inspired the curvy light fixture above. OVERLEAF: An almost-1970s aesthetic cozies up an outsized sitting room—with a gold velvet sofa, boldly patterned pillows, and chests painted in a playful, woodsy faux-bois motif.

Displayed alongside the limestone mantel, wooden curios take cues from the dense forest just outside. Adding more bohemian chic: an ultraplush rug woven in Morocco, a vintage abstract painting above the fireplace, and a sinuous sling chair in glove leather.

Make your bedroom a sanctuary, your own little retreat. It's like putting your oxygen mask on first before assisting other passengers, and it's vital for renewing your soul.

A Fortuny light fixture washes this bedroom in a soft glow, while caramel-rimmed agate lamps frame the gilt canopy bed. Ombré velvet curtains in ivory and pale blue and grass cloth wallcovering with a dreamy reflective sheen finish set a glamorous tone for this parental retreat.

OPPOSITE: Prepping for the day at a proper dressing table becomes an Old Hollywood experience when you can perch on a seat topped in snow-white fur. Adding to the luxury, the white leather-clad dressing table's drawers are edged in brass detailing. ABOVE: A Greek key border on the floors and custom brass legs on the vanities give this bathroom bespoke detailing that will stand the test of time.

For children, little inspires more than a map of the world, helping them plot out their many dreams and escapades to come. Their rooms should be magical little worlds where the imagination can run unchecked.

Start children on the monogram train early. In the son's bedroom, bold patterns from the bedding and the curtains create a lively energy to match his sparkling personality. One of my go-to classics for the younger gents—Pendleton's Glacier National Park blanket—dresses the bed.

Building on the well-traveled theme in this dreamy domicile: a chest of drawers that calls to mind antique steamer trunks of yore. A whimsical convex mirror surrounded by sharpened No. 2 pencils hangs in easy view from the bed.

What's more inviting to a young child than a nook that's just their size? OPPOSITE: In this nursery, a palette of pink, red, and white welcomes this baby to the world in style. Wild hares race around the room on a fanciful wallcovering and a bold, graphic rug keeps it all from being too sweet. I caution against designing nurseries that are too saccharine, reminding my clients that babies grow real personalities in a short time and need a room to match.

Going Graphic

Adding a graphic element to a room is like using salt when cooking your favorite dish: without it, the flavors can be lackluster, but with just the right amount, the dish comes alive. People often ask me, "Do you start your interior designs from the rug, or do you start from the ceiling and work down?" We often begin by finding a driving force to take center stage, such as a powerhouse light fixture—intentionally oversized for dramatic effect—or patterned tile floors with strong geometry, or a favorite painting or sculpture that sets your pulse racing. It may require a leap of faith, but going for gusto with scale, pattern, color, and contrast can truly transform a space.

Bold choices are also just plain logical in rooms built for drama, like those with soaring ceilings or powerful millwork. In one living room I recently designed (overleaf), a modern painting and a light fixture ringed by fabric tassels steal the spotlight, while the rest of the space is restrained. It's a lesson in what isn't there: no gallery wall and no bevy of small side tables. While it's certainly fully furnished, there's not a lot of fluff and everything has a purpose. If I'd chosen a more mundane light fixture and quieter art, it would still be a handsome room, but it wouldn't be an event. In the home of a different client, I searched the house room by room to pull together her collection of botanicals, which had wandered everywhere from the bedroom to the garage. Now they hang in unison within black frames along an open staircase; the divergent botanicals play off one another, and their differences come to light.

In this home for an artist, a doctor, and their children, I upped the drama in the dining space and took advantage of the generous ceiling height by installing an overscale iron fixture (hung in relation to the room, as opposed to the dining table). An oval table is encircled by black klismos chairs. Hanging in view above the fireplace, an antique Chinese robe invites further investigation.

In the living room of this family compound in Richmond, an earthy palette of camel, black, and white keeps the bold choices in sync. The organic profile of the coffee table nestles snugly into a sectional sofa, a commissioned William McLure abstract painting hangs above the fireplace, and fringed tassels encircle the light fixture.

The strong geometry of the Beni Ourain rug grounds this home's airy foyer.
OPPOSITE: Next to the streamlined sofa, shagreen end tables and sculptural lamps
let guests know right from the start that this art-loving home is full of surprises.

I'm often associated with colorful interiors, but some of my favorite spaces have resulted from designing with a very limited use of color—which allows subtler elements to come front and center.

Sometimes these graphic touches can be veritable magic tricks, sleights of hand meant to deceive the eye. Take black: it's our strongest non-color, and it always packs a punch. I often use it to outline windows or doorways, drawing an exclamation point around a view. Pattern is another one of our favorite attention-grabbing design tools. If you want to dip your toes into using pattern with a wallpaper, fabric, or floor material, remember that motifs in black, white, and gray tend to wear well over time. And while it may seem counterintuitive, large-scale versions feel correct in large rooms and make small rooms feel even larger. So, when in doubt, just go big. Before clients commit to a print, we always tell them to take it home, drive around in their car with it, or tack it up next to their bed. After living with it for a couple of weeks, they'll know if it's the right fit.

In a room with strong graphic elements, practicing restraint is essential. One would think you could go full throttle, but it's important to find the limit. Too many graphic pieces can cloud the vision of a room. Using bold interior pieces is similar to accessorizing with a statement necklace. It doesn't work with a patterned top, but put it on with a simple strapless black gown, and wow.

An Akari lantern floats above the dining table with an ethereal, moonlike quality, and the Lucite table boosts the room's airy impression. A series of paintings installed horizontally at eye level maximizes visibility.

A curved foyer wall is home to an equally curvaceous settee, upholstered in a colorful floral crewel fabric. The abstract painting is by artist Frankie Slaughter. OPPOSITE: The client's collection of pressed botanicals becomes even more eye-catching when grouped on this gallery wall in their pretty pink-stucco Greek Revival. OVERLEAF: Double-stacked windows are perfectly scaled with this kitchen's elevated ceilings; also generously scaled, the hand-plastered range hood melds fluidly into the wall.

OPPOSITE: Staggered bird's nest prints echo the lines of the custom banquette in this wet bar seating arrangement. ABOVE: Industrial marble pendant lights, a vanity wrapped in a living brass finish, and a trio of diminutive sculptures make stepping into the powder room of this contemporary home an artful experience. OVERLEAF: Gauzy curtains are offset by black doors and window sashes in this airy sunroom. A jute rug, a coffee table wrapped in twine, and open-weave rattan chairs add to the fuss-free, kick-off-your-heels vibe.

High-performance fabrics allow the sectional sofa in this pool house to welcome barefoot lounging in damp bathing suits. OPPOSITE: For a tactile client, texture was vital in this alpine bedroom in the Blue Ridge Mountains, from the densely piled rug, to the pom-pom–edged throw and the laser-cut cowhide banding at the bed rail's edge. The mother-of-pearl inlaid nightstands were made in India.

Contemporary

A RIVERFRONT RETREAT

T here's a problem with vacation homes: eventually you're forced to leave them and return to your normal life. Not so at this property that hugs the James River, where the water wends from dam to isle, punctuated by rushing rapids. When my clients first walked into the house, they said it had the feel of a getaway retreat. Their first thought was: "Wouldn't it be wonderful to live in your vacation home year-round?" We approached the interiors with the goal of creating an endless holiday.

We found all of our design inspiration in an ancient muse: the surrounding landscape. Nature has no hard angles, no plumb lines. So, we began by selecting shapes that had soft edges and curves, connecting to the riverside vista afforded by the abundant glass walls. A large room like this home's forty-eight-foot-long main living space—dubbed "the river room"—has a tendency to feel unapproachable and cold, so we worked hard to cozy it up from the beginning. We created separate, intimate seating areas. On one side of the room, a duo of chaises face each other, forming a tête-a-tête with a view. On the other side of the room, a fireside sectional is generous enough in scale to accommodate the whole family. Above the mantel, a bentwood walnut sculpture lends an earthy nod to the adjacent oaks and longleaf pines just in view. Between the seating areas, a counter-height table and a hand-cut cocoa shell chandelier divide the room. The table offers a riverfront view for dining, a generous surface for family puzzle

When you're employing a neutral color palette, varying finishes is essential for creating visual interest. PRECEDING: A ribbon-like light fixture echoes the round antique table in the foyer. OVERLEAF: In grisaille tones, scenic wallpaper imitates the property's own wooded setting and water views. The age-old bench and antique giltwood mirror supply a heady dose of history in the clean-lined architecture.

When floor-to-ceiling windows overlook nature's leafy splendor, organic upholstery choices and finishes—like wool bouclé and unvarnished woods—are a must for creating a warm, layered look. The abstract bentwood sculpture hung above the fireplace was a commission by artist Jeremy Holmes.

I kept the palette simple in this living space, limiting color to the autumnal hues of the velvet throw pillows, to center attention to the James River views. OVERLEAF: A counter-height table divides the expansive forty-eight-foot-long riverside room into two clearly defined spaces.

In a room with floor-to-ceiling glass walls and a killer view, clean-lined pieces were a must. Try as you might, you'll never upstage Mother Nature, so I politely acquiesced and gave her the leading role.

night, and a central location for a cocktail-hour command center. A wide, framed opening in the river room offers easy access to an elegantly appointed kitchen.

Whenever designing a kitchen, I try to use streamlined design components. With all the accoutrements needed for day-to-day cooking and dining, kitchens beg to be cluttered. We channeled serenity in this kitchen and camouflaged refrigerators, freezers, and other large appliances behind bench-made, limewashed cabinetry that is adorned with hardware that charms like a flash of bespoke jewelry. The custom-fabricated brass range hood has a living finish that will patina over time, lending burnished magnetism. The pendant lights' gold-leaf interiors cast a soft, flattering glow.

To hold the focus on the view, we kept the color palette of the interior mostly muted and natural with cloud-grays, whites, and blonds that conjure flaxen grasses catching the sunlight. For the inner reception room, I selected a scenic wallcovering that echoes the banks of the nearby James River. In shades of black, white, and gray, it complements without distracting, and tempers the gilding of the eighteenth-century French mirror. In the river room, throw pillows supply the pumpkin-spice hues of a Virginia autumn in golds and rich apricots. Varying upholstery textures, from cashmere to linen to a nubby bouclé, become even more important in a neutral space, giving the tonal interiors the low-key layered effect of pebbles on a riverbank.

An antique stool from a favorite *antiquaire*, Kim Faison Antiques, with turned wood legs and original mustard-yellow tassels, is a historical counterpoint to the modernist chaise.
OVERLEAF: This clean-lined kitchen puts the focus on glimmering brass details. With most of the appliances hidden behind limewashed cabinetry, the workhorse space feels tranquil and elegant.

Why shouldn't necessities be as beautiful as they are functional?
Form definitely rivals function in this range hood that I had fabricated
in brass, its unlacquered finish guaranteed to mellow over time.
OPPOSITE: Through arched passageways, the adjacent dining room beckons.

In such a vibrant and natural setting, this home's driving design force was an organic aesthetic. But I added elegant notes and refined gold finishes throughout to take things to another level of chic.

A gold-leaf twig chandelier by Julie Neill mirrors the natural wonderland beyond the dining room windows— albeit with a dash of luxury. I leave blond floors bare when possible to give rooms a sense of Scandinavian calm.

In an entry framed by steel windows and doors, an abstract painting hangs above a stone demilune table. OPPOSITE: Poolside, lightweight woven dining chairs optically balance a cast-stone dining table topped with a basket of free-ranging hydrangeas. OVERLEAF: A curvaceous outdoor sofa and sculptural woven chairs reflect Mother Nature's free-form shapes.

The Magic of the Mix

I've long been besotted with the houses and garden follies of a designer many have never heard of: Furlow Gatewood. After decades in New York City as an antiques dealer, the nonagenarian decamped to Americus, Georgia, and began creating a dreamland for his own enjoyment. As you survey his interiors, your eye passing over Gothic marble mantel ornaments, porcelain birds, and cotton-slipcovered Georgian armchairs, it's clear he is a master of the mix. A single room in one of his houses has a lifetime of stories to tell; you just want to dive in and stay.

So, when I think about what my own stock-in-trade is, the magic of the mix always comes to mind. I strive to combine the old and new, knowing that the juxtaposition of the *differences* is what shows the individual pieces to better advantage. It's like a secret potion where every distinct element comes together in perfect harmony—colors, finishes, and furniture with patina alongside the sleek and new. I enjoy visiting historic houses where rooms are preserved in their particular epochs down to the very last detail, but would I ever want to live that way? No. Evolution is happening every minute in design, and so many products are better than their predecessors. Yet I love a reference to the past, and the craftsmanship that went into so many antiques and vintage pieces of furniture.

Without a good mix, rooms fall flat. With it, you're intrigued. Envision a room from a perch on a crisp white sofa. It takes a minute to notice the pair of silk brocade–dressed Louis XVI armchairs, the carved eighteenth-century Spanish trunk across from you, and the long-haired Moroccan rug from the 1970s under your toes. A contemporary abstract painting dominates a large wall, but it may be an intriguing century-old portrait in an ornate frame

In a Virginia country house, antiques are all but required. Here, an Oushak rug and the client's own collection of antique maps impart a storied feel, made modern with contemporary art and a bergère chair upholstered in graphic silk fabric.

The perfect patina on this extravagantly detailed eighteenth-century settee becomes all the more sexy and unassuming when stripped to its original muslin and upholstery tacks. OPPOSITE: A seventeenth-century painted Gustavian wall screen introduces a burst of crisp Swedish blue that's mirrored by the adjacent antique tea table.

The client's stash of Rose Medallion china takes pride of place in the living room of their country home. Lending the space a necessary modernity: a pair of sculptural table lamps. Silk curtains, velvet upholstery, and a Turkish rug unite in the client's favorite color, salmon.

In my own guest room, I employed vintage textiles as a bed throw and a statement-making bed hanging in lieu of a headboard. OPPOSITE: Antique silhouettes from Switzerland and transferware plates become a de facto gallery wall.

that captures your eye. That's how it works in a room with a mix. It grabs you on multiple levels. Take the dining room within this chapter, which peacocks as much as inanimate objects can. In the evening, a gold light fixture I had made in Marrakech washes geometric patterns across the de Gournay wallpaper. A tailored blond dining table is surrounded by square-backed Italian dining chairs, the backs upholstered in contrasting quilted gold velvet. Ecru wool curtain panels are edged with a sinuous gold band, and an eighteenth-century half-sunburst illuminates the mantel. In another space, I showcased my client's collection of antique delftware vases by grouping them on one wall. A modern coffee table and gilded end tables reminiscent of palm trunks give edge to an otherwise traditional space. It's a curated look—and it's definitely not a room that was purchased off the showroom floor.

Still, it's rare that I have a client who isn't a tad overwhelmed by how to get the mix right. It offers them great comfort when I say, "Just trust me, I know." I think I was blessed with an innate sense of how to achieve balance in a room, but my instinctual sensibility about how to make the mix is a craft I have honed by just doing it—experimenting and rearranging and editing and adding back in. Admittedly, it takes time. But doesn't everything worth doing?

Collections become even more powerful when they can be seen together. Here, I placed antique Delft faience vases atop wall brackets in varying shapes to add interest. The coffee table was custom made in a taller height, a visual trick that puts it more in scale with the sky-high ceilings of this Greek Revival house.

In a Federal-era row house in Richmond, original moldings set the tone for elegance. Bringing things into the modern era: color punches of breezy yellow on white with notes of steadying teal, such as in the midcentury chair at left. The abstract painting is by Karen Blair. OVERLEAF: The walls of hand-painted golden peacocks in this dining room glimmer after dark, thanks to the glow cast by a light fixture made in Marrakech. Atop the mantel, an eighteenth-century half-sunburst.

An antique Swedish settee frames one end of the dining room and has an unlikely neighbor in a totem sculpture by Julie Silvers framed by scalloped curtains. Backs of Louis XVI-style dining chairs repeat the pop of color. OPPOSITE: A nineteenth-century commode in tulipwood, with kingwood marquetry inlay.

In this sunny solarium in Virginia, a daybed is placed for a prime view of the expansive lawn. The sculptural chairs are woven in leather. OPPOSITE: I installed a cozy banquette for games and puzzles galore. Overhead, the pair of bubble glass chandeliers casts a magical glow befitting a garden scene.

Soulful

A HISTORIC HOMESTEAD

T his Richmond home has an old soul, and I mean that literally. When my client—a meditation teacher—first visited it with her realtor, she felt that there was a presence at the door. She also sensed this spirit was anxious about her entering. She researched the house and discovered that it was built in 1743 in the bucolic countryside near Amelia, Virginia. It was moved to its current location in the city of Richmond in 1927. Learning of a former owner named Miss Lizzie, my client began to think her spirit was lingering there. When my client and her husband eventually bought the property, she went inside and spoke to the walls: "I'm going to take such good care of this house, and you are always welcome here—it will always be your home." Miss Lizzie must have been satisfied, because the project progressed without a hitch.

A grande dame of this age isn't without her flaws. The house served as a boys' school during World War I, and some of the other potential buyers felt that the interior of the house was forbidding, thanks in part to its burly woodwork. Rather than attempt to conventionally lighten it up by whitewashing the woodwork and covering windows and furnishings with pale, quiet colors, we decided to fight brawn with brawn. We painted most of the walls a knocked-down white, a color we hand-tinted on-site with a hint of umber to make it quieter on the eye. It struck the perfect moody chord. Dramatic floor-to-ceiling curtains dress the windows, gray velvet in the dining room and pumpkin silk in the living room. While both curtain fabrics are

In this Virginia historic home, a curated mix of furniture, frames, and objets d'art in various finishes have an appealing strength against the original woodwork. PRECEDING, FROM LEFT: hand-woven Charleston baskets ornament a foyer's original curio cabinet. In the entrance hall, a contemplative wall color sets the stage for colorful Moroccan rugs.

Age is just a number, especially in a gallery wall. Modern art can marry centuries-old antique pieces and live happily together.

historic colors that have endured for centuries, they feel fresh, bold, and in perfect harmony with the architectural millwork. In the library, we painted the bookcases a deep teal to showcase the gold and red spines of the collected antique tomes displayed there. Keeping the design powerful and the colors rich paired seamlessly with the architecture, giving the home a zen sensibility.

Soaring twelve-foot-high ceilings provided ample space for the homeowners' extensive art collection, which is hung salon-style, as if at the Louvre. With such a large collection, I grouped the artwork according to genre. The dining room became a gallery devoted to female portraits, the main bedroom a calming huddle of pastoral scenes. Creating a gallery wall is one of my favorite art installations. First, I plan it out on the floor, looking at the composition from above on a ladder, and make small adjustments until it feels right. Then, I use painter's tape to outline the exact placement on the wall. I like to avoid symmetry, but it's important to maintain a sense of balance. Pro tip: I almost never put the biggest piece in the middle of a gallery wall, instead offsetting it slightly to the left or right. If you create balance, your eye will be able to enjoy every piece. Frames require their own equilibrium. I like a little bit of bling, like mellowed gold frames, paired with something more modest, like an unframed canvas. And if starting your own art collection, my advice is to buy what you love. Though significant, the pedigree of a piece is not the most important factor. If a work of art appeals to your soul, you'll always be able to incorporate it into your home.

An art collection that runs the gamut from street art to fine century-old paintings delights the eye. PRECEDING: The casual sisal rug and hemp-rope coffee table help balance important antiques with a lighter touch, combining formality with informality for a more bohemian feel.

FACE of an ISLAND

Dramatic floor-to-ceiling curtains set a luxurious tone. OPPOSITE: As the mother of three girls, the homeowner champions girl power in her collection of female portraits. OVERLEAF: A secondary seating area within the dining room helps create a more casual air in the space, with Italian gilt chairs upholstered in cheeky eyelash fabric.

To achieve an evolved look, layer multiple patterns and textures. I encourage diving in headfirst. Go for the gusto at the start—the edits can come later.

To help counteract the heaviness of the home's woodwork, we used a mix of high and low in the decor—not unlike my client's habit of wearing diamond earrings with her yoga pants. Mixing textures is also key to a layered, timeless look. Here, Charleston sweetgrass baskets pop from within a curio cabinet, balancing ornate antiques with a lighter touch. In the entry hall, colorful Moroccan rugs add exuberant color while the walls remain quiet. In the living room, linen sofas, natural fiber pillows, and a round hemp-rope table are casually nonchalant, while glowing silk curtains and tall ceilings feel inherently formal.

We refrained from altering much of the home's architecture; I have great respect for a beautiful, centuries-old house. But our goal was to transform it from a somber house into a welcoming home, and that meant reconsidering the modestly scaled doors on the main level. We replaced them with big cased openings along the entry hall that allow light to flow and invite you into each room. I have a hunch Miss Lizzie would approve.

With walls and ceilings wrapped in texture-rich grass cloth, the keeping room off the galley kitchen is a cozy multitasking spot. PRECEDING: Wallpapering the comparatively sleek kitchen (and its ceiling) served to separate it from the adjacent keeping room. OVERLEAF: A topsy-turvy stacked-ball table is an invigorating setting for morning coffee. The unbridled mix of fabrics—including embroideries, ikats, and Fortuny damasks—adds to the room's rich bohemian aura. A bay window seat is accented with pewter-gray trim, framing the forest beyond the glass.

In good, old houses—the ones that hold so much history of lives lived and memories made—it's important to know when to step back, stop designing, and let the house tell its own story.

The stair's newel post was discovered to be older than the house itself. It still has the errant carvings from days long ago, when the building served as a school for boys. OVERLEAF: I painted the library walls and bookcases a rich aqua-blue that allows the red and gold spines of antique tomes to pop.

In the bedroom, a cluster of paintings capturing far-flung ports of call envelops the headboard. At the foot of the bed sits an Italian bench upholstered in pony hide for a brazen burst of fun.

Acknowledgments

Five years ago, my friend and client Mollie asked, "So when are you doing your book?" After a long pause, I answered honestly that I hadn't really thought about a book. But the wheels definitely started spinning that day and I began to imagine my individual design projects as more of a cohesive unit of work.

Enter Christina Juarez, my sage and trusted counsel on public relations. She helped to convince me that my point of view and body of work was distinctive enough to support a book. The task of translating my design aesthetic into a thoughtfully woven narrative thread was done masterfully by my gifted book agent, Jill Cohen. Jill and her team helped me to navigate the publishing process and I couldn't have been in more capable hands. Doug Turshen and Steve Turner provided skilled art direction and good-naturedly experimented with all of my suggestions. Kathryn O'Shea-Evans helped me turn my disorganized, albeit prolific ramblings into erudite thoughts and stories ripe with imagery that made my words come alive. As deadlines loomed, my editor, Jenny Florence, provided a cool, calm presence and I am forever thankful for her and the team at The Monacelli Press who believed in me, my work, and the value of what I have to share.

There is no book without a portfolio of projects and the images here represent the supportive clients who have made my book a reality. Our collaborations have resulted in great fun, greater friendships, and I've loved dressing your houses into individualistic and welcoming homes. It is surely the sum of my body of work that has landed me here and my heartfelt thanks go to each of those clients whose homes are featured here, and also to all the clients along the way who believed in me. You've given me the greatest gift of all by being happy at home.

It quickly becomes evident when reading this book that my family has provided me bounteous inspiration. They are also an incredibly supportive group. My husband, John, has always given me infinite encouragement in my design career and made himself available for thoughtful editorial feedback about my book, at all hours of the day and night. And to my children, John and Steph, Robert and Jenna, Pierre and Ashton, Swain, and Isabel, you have been right beside me the whole time, bringing my design magazine features to show-and-tell, knowing the difference in thread counts before your multiplication tables, and always politely humoring me as we quickly pulled off the road when I spotted yet another rusty ANTIQUES sign.

During the peak of mothering this busy group, I drove five carpools a day and attended enough athletic events that an Excel spreadsheet shaped the daily schedule. Back then, I was blessed with a business partner who kept our collective feet in the door in the design world. My friend Deborah Valentine and I schlepped our children and wallpaper books through thick and thin. She's moved on from the design world, but remains one of the most creative design inspirations I have.

I wake up on a workday, happy and eager to drive the short distance to my office. I am one of the lucky ones, loving what I do for a living. To be greeted by my fun-loving and invincible team is the icing on the cake. To Logan, Emily, Tammy, Martha, and Jane: thank you for being so brilliant at your jobs. And to Kate Stikeleather and Robyn Framme, beloved friends and talented designers, who both finish my sentences, we've already had an amazing journey together and I know even more fun is around the corner. This really is *our* book.

In appreciation for all the houses I've dressed and the memories they hold.

Photography Credits

Mali Azima: 6, 42, 44–47, 50–51, 58–59, 61–65, 67–69, 71–73, 75–94, 96–103, 125, 127–33, 135–37, 139, 140–43, 145–47, 149, 150–53, 156–57, 196, 198–201, 212–13, 239

Kip Dawkins: 48–49, 121, 163, 166, 168–169, 205

Gordon Gregory: 2, 4–5, 10, 12–13, 15–19, 25–27, 29, 31–33, 36–37, 40–41, 53–57, 105–107, 109–120, 122–24, 155, 158–59, 161–62, 164–65, 167, 170–73, 175–83, 185–89, 191–95, 202–203, 206–11

Tasha Tolliver: 9

Bjorn Wallander: 20, 22–23, 35, 38–39

Luke White: 214–15, 217–19, 221–27, 229–32, 234–37

Library of Congress Control Number: 2021931643

ISBN 978-1-58093-580-7

Developed in collaboration with Jill Cohen Associates, LLC.

Design by Doug Turshen with Steve Turner

Printed in China

Monacelli
A Phaidon Company
65 Bleecker Street
New York, NY 10012
www.monacellipress.com